AUTHOR OF THE *NEW YORK TIMES* BESTSELLER
INFINITE POSSIBILITIES

MIKE DOOLEY

NOTES *FROM THE* UNIVERSE

PERPETUAL FLIP CALENDAR

D1770025

About *Notes from the Universe*

What started in 1998 as an email sent out weekly to 38 addresses has since blossomed into today's daily *Notes from the Universe*, sent to over 350,000 subscribers in 189 countries. Brand new *Notes* are still being written by Mike Dooley and are sent out every weekday. To receive your free, personalized *Notes* go to www.tut.com to sign up!

Plus, there's lots more at tut.com...

Join the fun, find travel buddies, create your own online vision board, connect with friends, and much more at **TUT's Adventurers Club**! Membership is free!

© 2010 by Mike Dooley

Published and distributed in the United States by:
TUT Enterprises, Inc. www.tut.com

All of the *Notes* in this calendar were written by Mike Dooley.

Editorial Supervision: Hope Koppelman

Designers: Paola Malicki & Vanessa An Lim

Artist: Heather Brady

All rights reserved. No part of this calendar may be reproduced by any mechanical, photographic, or electronic process, or in the form of a phonographic recording; nor may it be stored in a retrieval system, transmitted, or otherwise be copied for public or private use—other than for "fair use" as brief quotations embodied in articles and reviews—without prior written permission of the publisher.

ISBN: 9780981460215

UPC: 660159004023

Printed in China

About the Author

Mike Dooley is a former PriceWaterhouseCoopers international tax consultant, turned entrepreneur. He is the founder of TUT's Adventurers Club, a philosophical club for the adventure of life. He's also the author of 8 books, including the *Notes from the Universe* series, the New York Times Bestseller *Infinite Possibilities: The Art of Living Your Dreams*, and he was one of the featured teachers in the international phenomenon, *The Secret*. Mike lives what he teaches, traveling internationally speaking to thousands on life, dreams, and happiness. To see his speaking schedule and find out more, visit us at www.tut.com.

 Also by Mike Dooley

- *Lost in Space*
- *Infinite Possibilities: The Art of Living Your Dreams*
- *Notes from the Universe, Books I, II, & III*
- *Totally Unique Thoughts: Reminders of Life's Everyday Magic*
- *Choose Them Wisely: Thoughts Become Things*
- *Leveraging the Universe and Engaging the Magic*
- *Manifesting Change: It Couldn't Be Easier*
- *Thoughts Become Things*

More inspirational novelty and gift items
can be found at www.tut.com

Introduction

If I told you there've been no mistakes, that I understand every decision you've ever made, and that the challenges you've faced, you've faced for everyone, would you listen?

If I told you that what you dream of, I dream of for you, that the only things "meant to be" are what you decide upon, and that all that stands between you and the life of your dreams are the thoughts you choose to think, would you try to understand?

And if I told you that you are never alone, that there are angels who sing your name in praise, and that I couldn't possibly be any more proud of you than I already am, would you believe me?

Would you? Even if I pulled your leg, made you blush, and winked between the lines?

Then I shall...

The Universe

YOU
ARE
ADORED!

JANUARY
ENERO
JANVIER

1

When in doubt, show up early. Think less.
Feel more. Ask once. Give thanks.
Expect the best. Appreciate everything.
Never give up. Make it fun. Lead.
Invent. Regroup. Wink. Chill. Smile.
And live as if your success was inevitable,
and so it shall be.

The Universe

© www.tut.com

DECEMBER
DICIEMBRE
DECEMBRE **31**

Ever wish for do-over days?
You know, hit the reset-button
and give 'er another shot?

Cool.

Will today work?

It's never too late,
The Universe

© www.tut.com

JANUARY
ENERO
JANVIER

2

What you want has no bearing on whether
or not you'll get it. None. Nada. Zippo.

It's only ever a question of whether or not you
can behave as if you already have it.

I got you, babe -
The Universe

© www.tut.com

DECEMBER
DICIEMBRE
DECEMBRE 30

Treating "any old job"
as if it were your dream job is the fastest way
to spark the kind of life changes
that will yield your dream job.

Same for any old house, friend, day, life,
or pair of espadrilles.

The Universe

© www.tut.com

JANUARY
ENERO
JANVIER

3

Folks are often so mesmerized by
gold medals, trophies, and the daunting heights
they aspire to, they tend to forget that
their heroes and heroines, more often than not,
started with far less than they now have.

You are poised for greatness.

The Universe

© www.tut.com

DECEMBER
DICIEMBRE
DECEMBRE **29**

Usually the most beautiful people,
the most popular and loved, the "in" and chic,
the cool and hip, are the last ones to ever wonder
about life, how it really works, manifesting change,
and making a difference.

You beat the system.

The Universe

© www.tut.com

You don't have to take everything so seriously.
Reality isn't black and white, answers aren't always
yes or no, and absolutely nothing has to happen today.
Act when you're ready. Be led by your feelings.
And the next time someone wants to fit you into
a mold, just tell 'em that your jeans are in the wash,
your angel's at the mall, and Oprah's on the other line.

The Universe

© www.tut.com

DECEMBER
DICIEMBRE
DECEMBRE 28

A tip on legend making:

Always do what you most want to do,
and do it your way.

The Universe

© www.tut.com

JANUARY
ENERO
JANVIER
5

Lots of things don't make sense at first
when only the physical senses are used.

What does your heart say?

Boom,
The Universe

© www.tut.com

DECEMBER
DICIEMBRE
DECEMBRE 27

Ever have the feeling that the whole world
is revolving around you?

Good, because I'd hate to think that
it went unnoticed.

The Universe

© www.tut.com

JANUARY
ENERO
JANVIER 6

If, once upon a time in your life, suddenly
and without warning, an event, a person, or some
unexpected good news suddenly changed everything
in your life for the better, it can only mean one thing...

Chances are astronomically high
that it will happen again.

The Universe

© www.tut.com

DECEMBER
DICIEMBRE
DECEMBRE
26

Adversity, challenges, and bumps in the road
are often the first signs that a great healing
has begun.

Thinking of you,
The Universe

Especially when one seeks to understand them.

© www.tut.com

JANUARY
ENERO
JANVIER

7

Investment Advice for Turbulent Times:
Kindness pays HUGE dividends,
materially and ethereally, forever and ever.

Love on,
The Universe

© www.tut.com

DECEMBER
DICIEMBRE
DECEMBRE 25

Lo and behold, before your very eyes,
and all around you, is a reflection of what lies within.

Glad we cleared that up.

The Universe

Exactly what you thought you'd see
and exactly where you thought you'd be, huh?

© www.tut.com

JANUARY
ENERO
JANVIER
8

Always, when you don't know what you want,
want happiness; and when you don't know
what to do, do anything.

You can start today -
The Universe

© www.tut.com

DECEMBER
DICIEMBRE
DECEMBRE 24

Please, don't ever settle for less
than what you really, really want.

I mean, what else am I going to do
with all this stuff?

The Universe

© www.tut.com

JANUARY
ENERO
JANVIER
9

Of course not everyone understands you.
It takes crazy to know crazy.
It takes sexy to know sexy.
And most assuredly, it takes cool to know cool.

Yeah, uh-huh, alright -
The Universe

It also takes great to know great.

© www.tut.com

DECEMBER
DICIEMBRE
DECEMBRE 23

Who would have ever thought

that you would see, feel, and intuitively know
so much that others completely miss?

Oh yeah, that was the whole point.

Had to be me -
The Universe

You've changed absolutely everything.

© www.tut.com

JANUARY
ENERO
JANVIER 10

Remember, the whole point of this "drill,"
besides the daily adventures, falling in love
over and over again, and the color purple,
was simply to give you a little vacation
from being Me.

You don't have to take everything so seriously.

The Universe

© www.tut.com

DECEMBER
DICIEMBRE
DECEMBRE 22

Asking "how" is pure, unadulterated,
low-energy, health-zapping, fun-squeezing,
party-pooping doubt.

Oh! So sorry! You said, "Wow!" My mistake.

As you were -
The Universe

© www.tut.com

JANUARY
ENERO
JANVIER
11

When you look around you at those in the world
who flourish, thrive, laugh, and love;
those whose lives are filled with friendships,
adventure, and abundance… aren't they,
more often than not, first and foremost, the dreamers?

You so have it made.

The Universe

© www.tut.com

DECEMBER
DICIEMBRE
DECEMBRE **21**

Most, including those who love you most,
have absolutely no idea of how much they depend
upon you to follow your dreams.

But they do.

You go -
The Universe

© www.tut.com

Wondering how else you could view life
when you're experiencing emotional pain
is a sign of spiritual maturity.

Wondering how else you could view life
when things are already going really well
is the sign of a spiritual rock star.

The Universe

© www.tut.com

DECEMBER
DICIEMBRE
DECEMBRE 20

You might not always see it, but everything,
always, plays to a greater good.

Things keep on getting better and better.

And you're already the kind of person
you once dreamed you'd become.

All choked up,
The Universe

© www.tut.com

JANUARY
ENERO
JANVIER 13

When in a hurry,
step #1 for changing the entire world,
is falling in love with it as it already is.

Same for changing yourself.

And best of all, with this approach,
there is no step #2.

The Universe

© www.tut.com

DECEMBER
DICIEMBRE
DECEMBRE
19

Sometimes, what's really cool
is giving profuse thanks for
the good fortunes that befall others
—no matter who they are—
because, invariably, your joy for them
will yield the same good fortunes for you.

The Universe

© www.tut.com

JANUARY
ENERO
JANVIER
14

The secret behind miracles is
that the person performing them begins
without any knowledge whatsoever of exactly
how they will succeed… yet still they begin.

When you move, I move -
The Universe

Once again, taking action saves the day.

© www.tut.com

DECEMBER
DICIEMBRE
DECEMBRE 18

Having preferences doesn't mean
you're judgmental. They just ensure that
as the winds of divinity are blown
through your heart...
the melody is unlike any other.

So have them. Have them BIG time.

The Universe

© www.tut.com

Appreciating what you have little of is easy.

Appreciating what you have lots and lots of
takes a spiritual master.

And you so have lots,
The Universe

So appreciating ALL of you.

© www.tut.com

DECEMBER
DICIEMBRE
DECEMBRE
17

You will be happy to know

that I have personally authorized the release of enough
joy into the atmosphere of your shiny, little planet
for every man, woman, and child, to last for eternity.

Yep. Did it just after it cooled from its
molten mass phase.

The Universe

© www.tut.com

JANUARY
ENERO
JANVIER 16

Whenever your perspective on something
creates emotional pain, it's always because
your perspective is still so narrow that you've
yet to see all the good it will make possible.

Because it will.

You can see clearly now...
The Universe

© www.tut.com

The answer is no. Absolutely not.

The question, of course, was:
"Are mistakes in time and space possible?"

The Universe

Nor is there any such thing as "lost time."

© www.tut.com

JANUARY
ENERO
JANVIER 17

The very feelings you're now feeling
—the good, the bad, and the confused—
are in large part why you chose this lifetime:
To simply feel them.

You are exactly where you should be.

The Universe

© www.tut.com

DECEMBER
DICIEMBRE
DECEMBRE 15

A tip for advanced souls on how
to "WOW" the glorious mortals in your life:
Say very, very little indeed.

And when asked if you agree with their views,
always say, "Mostly."

WOW,
The Universe

© www.tut.com

JANUARY
ENERO
JANVIER 18

The greatest gift a parent can give a child
is the ability to become independently happy.

And the greatest gift a child can give a parent
is exercising that ability.

Happily,
The Universe

© www.tut.com

DECEMBER
DICIEMBRE
DECEMBRE

14

Be led by joy.

It's the whole point.

The Universe

Remember, before this entire adventure began,
you asked me to remind you of this?

© www.tut.com

JANUARY
ENERO
JANVIER 19

The reason things always work out for the best
is because this is actually the highest
of all spiritual laws.

Any apparent exceptions are simply evidence
that work is still in progress,
whether or not it can be seen.

The Universe

© www.tut.com

DECEMBER
DICIEMBRE
DECEMBRE 13

You wondering "how,"
is as silly as me wondering "why."

I don't, and neither should you.

I mean, let's not be that silly -
The Universe

You can have whatever you want if
you let me deliver it however I want.

© www.tut.com

JANUARY
ENERO
JANVIER **20**

Contrary to what would seem like logical thinking,
putting up your defenses actually inspires others
to put up their offenses.

En garde,
The Universe

The truly defenseless need no defense,
if you know what I mean.

© www.tut.com

DECEMBER
DICIEMBRE
DECEMBRE 12

Basically, getting what you want
is most efficiently accomplished
by pretending you already have it.

All of the time.

The Universe

Goodness, you've been laughing and smiling
a lot lately, haven't you?!

© www.tut.com

JANUARY
ENERO
JANVIER 21

The only way to get what you really want is
to know what you really want. The only way to know
what you really want is to know yourself.
The only way to know yourself is to be yourself.
And the only way to be yourself
is to listen to your heart.

I do,
The Universe

© www.tut.com

DECEMBER
DICIEMBRE
DECEMBRE
11

Sometimes difficult people are placed
on your path so that you can be reminded of
what you may have once put others through.

In all cases, you both thought it was a good
idea to meet up this time, for reasons that
will one day make perfect sense.

The Universe

© www.tut.com

JANUARY
ENERO
JANVIER 22

One of the most comforting thoughts of all
is knowing that all roads lead "home."

Even more comforting, is understanding
that you never left.

From all of us "back" home,
The Universe

© www.tut.com

DECEMBER
DICIEMBRE
DECEMBRE
10

If a bird that could fly
only wished for flight as it sat on a limb…
before long it would be unable to fly.

Same goes for anyone wishing for anything…
if all they do is wish.

The Universe

© www.tut.com

JANUARY
ENERO
JANVIER 23

The only person who should ever have to live
by your standards… is you.

Let everyone else off the hook.
Besides, it's doubtful they've lived as much,
dreamt as big, or will ever be able to saunter
quite like you.

The Universe

© www.tut.com

DECEMBER
DICIEMBRE
DECEMBRE
9

Just because you can have it all,
doesn't mean there's something wrong with you
until you do.

To the contrary, the simple fact that you stand
before such infinite possibilities, irrefutably means
that you are one bad mamma jamma.

That's a good thing,
The Universe

© www.tut.com

JANUARY
ENERO
JANVIER 24

Always keep in mind that no matter what has happened, you did the very best you could.

And so did those who may have let you down.

Great Love,
The Universe

© www.tut.com

DECEMBER
DICIEMBRE
DECEMBRE

8

A reassuring glance to an unsuspecting stranger
—across a room, down a hallway, or through a window—
can literally change the world, forever.

Even though it was pretty cool to begin with.

The Universe

© www.tut.com

JANUARY
ENERO
JANVIER 25

What if you were to see your every action
and inaction in this life so far, your every strength
and weakness, your every hope and fear,
as proof of your divinity?

We do.

The Universe

You've been simply amazing.

© www.tut.com

DECEMBER
DICIEMBRE
DECEMBRE

7

Got any good ideas for this week?

I'm thinking that anything can happen.

But, then, of course, it's not about what I think.

The Universe

I so love your continuum. It's so responsive,
versatile, and dependable. Kind of like chocolate.

JANUARY
ENERO
JANVIER 26

Do you ever wonder

whether you're on the right path?
Do you sometimes feel vulnerable in new relationships?
Does certainty elude you when big decisions loom?

Outstanding! Fantastic! Because so have all
the other legends who came before you.

The Universe

© www.tut.com

DECEMBER
DICIEMBRE
DECEMBRE
6

You can have what you want,
do what you dream, and brave what you fear,
if you first see it done in your mind.

Always works.

Always,

The Universe

And truly, your imagination is world class.
Although just which "world" is still being hotly debated.

© www.tut.com

JANUARY
ENERO
JANVIER
27

Always listen to your doubts.

Not just because they might teach you
of your fears, but because, sometimes,
they might teach you of your wisdom.

The Universe

© www.tut.com

DECEMBER
DICIEMBRE
DECEMBRE

5

Fear always goes away once two things
are realized: First, you're a spiritual being.
Second, nothing can ever be lost or taken from
a spiritual being that cannot be recreated;
not pride, nor money, nor love.

The Universe

© www.tut.com

Let the truth be your greatest source of comfort.
Because therein lies every possibility, hope,
and second chance one could ever imagine.

Not to mention the truths about who you are,
all you've achieved, and how much
you're already loved.

The Universe

© www.tut.com

DECEMBER
DICIEMBRE
DECEMBRE
4

Oh boy, are you ever going to laugh
when you find out you were perfect all along.

The Universe

Yes, "briefly." A very brief laugh.
Your lips will barely part and it's doubtful
anything will be heard.

© www.tut.com

JANUARY
ENERO
JANVIER 29

Any and all forms of separation, disconnects,
divides, partings, breakups, and goodbyes
are temporary. Very.

You'll be together far, far longer
than you will ever be apart.

Forever and ever -
The Universe

© www.tut.com

DECEMBER
DICIEMBRE
DECEMBRE

3

Funny, most folks "there"
are waiting for a sign of sorts from folks "here,"
before they make a move, take action, or commit.

Same "here."

The Universe

Good thing we have eternity, huh?

© www.tut.com

JANUARY
ENERO
JANVIER 30

This just in... No matter how happy
you have ever been, even at your happiest,
it won't come close to how happy
you will one day be.

Trust me, I'm there now...

The Universe

© www.tut.com

DECEMBER
DICIEMBRE
DECEMBRE

2

Today, we're going to make manifesting
dreams really, really easy.

There.

Now you just go have a ball.

We love you so much,
The Universe

© www.tut.com

JANUARY
ENERO
JANVIER 31

This year will not be just another year.
It's the absolute richest I've ever imagined,
with the most possibilities I've ever offered,
for the coolest people I've ever known
to do the greatest things ever done.

Set the bar high.

The Universe

© www.tut.com

DECEMBER
DICIEMBRE
DECEMBRE

1

What you see with your eyes is never
as important as what exists out of view.

Know what I'm talking about?

The Universe

And there is always so much more to see.

© www.tut.com

FEBRUARY
FEBRERO
FEVRIER

1

I'd say the biggest decision of your life was not
your career, your marital status, or your home...
it was choosing to love as often as you have.

And that's a lot,
The Universe

Especially when it seemed in vain (it never is).

© www.tut.com

NOVEMBER
NOVIEMBRE
NOVEMBRE 30

There is no choice you've ever made,
nor any you will ever make, that will limit you
as much as you may fear.

Nor even limit you at all.

How cool is that?
The Universe

Fear not, there have been no mistakes.

© www.tut.com

FEBRUARY
FEBRERO
FEVRIER

2

The courage to wonder

about other life-perspectives than presently held,
especially when they may contradict lifelong
convictions, takes not only a spiritual giant with
a child's curiosity, but a blazing desire for
more of everything life has to offer.

The Universe

© www.tut.com

The need to clarify, explain, or justify oneself
in personal relationships is always self-serving.

What's important is knowing the truth about why
you felt the need, because it often points to insecurities
that could be dealt with in more effective ways.

The Universe

© www.tut.com

Tip for the Advanced Metaphysician:
To begin living like you've never lived before,
begin living like you've never lived before.

There.

The Universe

Today is good for me.

© www.tut.com

NOVEMBER
NOVIEMBRE
NOVEMBRE 28

Talking a lot about something that bothers you
is a pretty good sign that you've got something huge
and profoundly liberating to learn.

The Universe

© www.tut.com

FEBRUARY
FEBRERO
FEVRIER

4

A goal or a dream that doesn't challenge
the dreamer to become more than they've ever been,
to go where they've never gone, and to feel things
they've never felt, is actually like wishing
for a giant life-snooze button.

Tacky.

The Universe

© www.tut.com

NOVEMBER
NOVIEMBRE
NOVEMBRE 27

It's not the size of your dreams
that determines whether or not they come true,
but the size of the actions you take
that implies their inevitable arrival.

Your greatest admirer,
The Universe

© www.tut.com

FEBRUARY
FEBRERO
FEVRIER

5

The best shortcut of all
to the life of your dreams,
is knowing that you've already arrived.

Because you have.

And by truly seeing this,
your "work" will be done.

The Universe

© www.tut.com

NOVEMBER
NOVIEMBRE
NOVEMBRE 26

Exactly where you've been
has made possible exactly who you are,
and I wouldn't change that for the world.

Clever thinking,
The Universe

© www.tut.com

FEBRUARY
FEBRERO
FEVRIER

6

All expenditures,
whether from the heart or the wallet,
in the past or present, big or small,
can be viewed as either
"depleting" or "enriching."

Enriching works for me.

The Universe

© www.tut.com

NOVEMBER
NOVIEMBRE
NOVEMBRE 25

Usually, it's not thinking about the bucks,
which makes one rich.

But thinking rich, which makes the bucks.

If you know what I mean.

Strut -
The Universe

© www.tut.com

FEBRUARY
FEBRERO
FEVRIER

7

The best way to find "love,"
which, incidentally, is just as true
for finding money, is to focus less on
these by-products of a life well lived
and more on a life well lived.

Simple is as simple does.

The Universe

© www.tut.com

NOVEMBER
NOVIEMBRE
NOVEMBRE **24**

Asking someone to change
is like pruning a tree;
neither will ever be the same again.

Scarier still, is that you can't quite know
in what new directions they'll grow.

The Universe

© www.tut.com

FEBRUARY
FEBRERO
FEVRIER

8

The thing that most forget while dreamily
looking off into the horizon for the ship of
their dreams is that such ships never sail in,
but are actually built beneath their very feet.

Ohh-wee-ohh,

The Universe

Get my drift?

© www.tut.com

NOVEMBER
NOVIEMBRE
NOVEMBRE 23

Do you know how to give folks
what they most, most, most want from you,
without even asking them what it is?

In all regards, *just be yourself.*

That's what they were after when they
manifested you into their lives.

You are, truly, one-of-a-kind -
The Universe

© www.tut.com

FEBRUARY
FEBRERO
FEVRIER
9

It is understandably human nature
to see yourself as small.

Until you stop seeing yourself as just human.

Should be easy for you...
The Universe

You are pure energy:
infinite, inexhaustible, and irresistible.

© www.tut.com

NOVEMBER
NOVIEMBRE
NOVEMBRE 22

Little else you say can change so much
in the life of another as words of praise,
compliments, or encouragement.

Way to go, beautiful -
The Universe

And remember that some of the best pats
on the back are the ones you give yourself.

© www.tut.com

FEBRUARY
FEBRERO
FEVRIER 10

If you understood the extraordinary gifts
that every single challenge in your life
makes possible, even inevitable,
you'd celebrate your challenges,
new and old alike, as the omens that they are
of new beginnings and spectacular change.

The Universe

© www.tut.com

NOVEMBER
NOVIEMBRE
NOVEMBRE 21

In virtually all person-to-person relationships,
disappointments can be lessened, setbacks can
be regained, and little annoyances can be
brushed off, when one stops and realizes
that such relationships are always temporary.

Physically speaking.

The Universe

© www.tut.com

If you could actually see the love
that at all times emanates from all people,
the first thing you'd likely think as anyone
came into view would be, "Behold, God."

Then you'd probably ask them how they do it.

The Universe

© www.tut.com

NOVEMBER
NOVIEMBRE
NOVEMBRE 20

Whenever in doubt, claim it all
—the good, the bad, and the ugly—
and your power will be restored.

The Universe

Responsibility is power.

© www.tut.com

I just can't think of anything
more important to tell you today
than *"Congratulations, outstanding, well done!"*

You are now, officially, the person
you once dreamed you'd become.

It always works,
The Universe

© www.tut.com

NOVEMBER
NOVIEMBRE
NOVEMBRE 19

Sure, you can always find prettier,
handsomer, skinnier, wiser, richer, younger, zippier.
But more often than not, one learns the most,
laughs the loudest, and smiles the widest
with those they've already found, especially
when they stop looking elsewhere.

The Universe

© www.tut.com

FEBRUARY
FEBRERO
FEVRIER

13

Learning to disassociate
your dream's manifestation from the illusions
that now surround you, to release yourself
from the burden of figuring out the "hows,"
and to trust what can't be seen,
are the high watermarks of
creative enlightenment.

The Universe

© www.tut.com

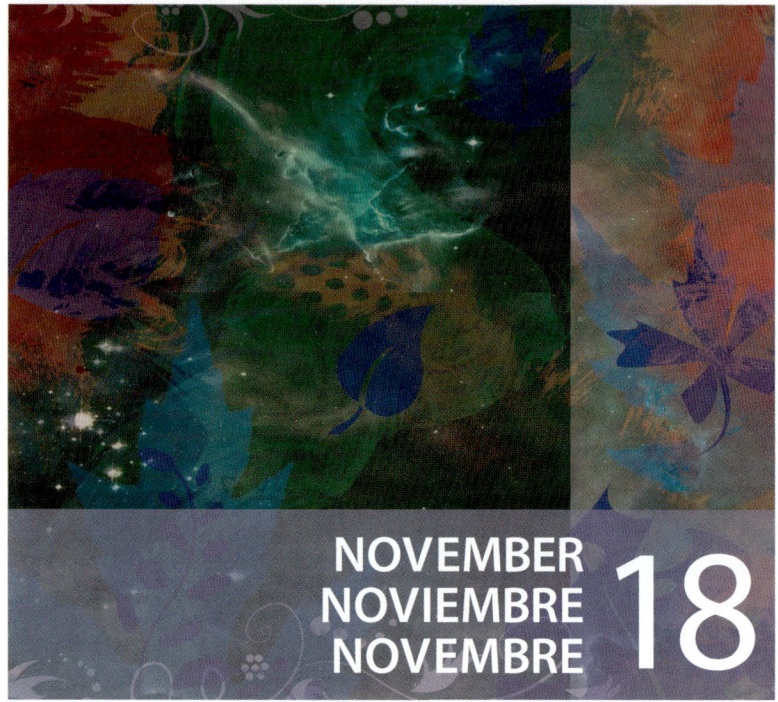

NOVEMBER
NOVIEMBRE
NOVEMBRE 18

It will "all" seem far easier
when you keep in mind, all of the time,
that it's supposed to be easy.

Everything.

That was easy,
The Universe

© www.tut.com

Some angels choose cleverly disguised
lives in time and space, just to help folks
get past judging by appearances.
No, they're not much to look at, listen to,
or dance with, and most would never guess
they're angels... but that's the point.

Every soul is beautiful.

The Universe

© www.tut.com

NOVEMBER
NOVIEMBRE
NOVEMBRE **17**

Never underestimate human spirit.

Especially not your own.

It comes from the finest stock,
if I do say so myself.

Be the ball,
The Universe

© www.tut.com

FEBRUARY
FEBRERO
FEVRIER
15

At the end of the day,
no matter how they behaved, no matter what
was said, and no matter how things turned out,
rest assured that your goodness will be known by all.

The Universe

© www.tut.com

NOVEMBER
NOVIEMBRE
NOVEMBRE 16

If you knew just how scared
most people are,
you'd be even braver.

Running faster, jumping higher,
and laughing louder.

The Universe

© www.tut.com

FEBRUARY
FEBRERO
FEVRIER 16

Some of the coolest dreams
that ever came true weren't dreams at all,
but standards that simply weren't compromised.

Always being your best, shining your brightest,
and standing as tall as you can,
pays far more dividends
than one might ever imagine.

The Universe

© www.tut.com

NOVEMBER
NOVIEMBRE
NOVEMBRE 15

Thinking is life's only variable.

Everything else was settled a long,
long time ago.

Sittin' pretty -
The Universe

© www.tut.com

Go way out.
Think beyond your present dreams,
to the dreams you will have once they've already
come true. And when you can clearly see
how confident you will walk
and how proud you will feel,
start walking and feeling like that today.

The Universe

© www.tut.com

NOVEMBER
NOVIEMBRE
NOVEMBRE 14

Those who are not yet spiritually wise,
simply cannot appreciate, or even recognize,
those who are.

Fortunately, you can still blow their socks off
as you live the truths you've uncovered.

Hubba, hubba -
The Universe

© www.tut.com

FEBRUARY
FEBRERO
FEVRIER
18

Have you noticed,
how lacking clarity is clarity itself?

How, if you aren't sure about something,
that alone, has meaning?

Honor uncertainty. It's the seed
from which all-knowingness comes.

The Universe

© www.tut.com

NOVEMBER
NOVIEMBRE
NOVEMBRE

13

Impatience is a sign of hurrying,
hurrying is a sign of worrying,
worrying is a sign of fear,
and fear is a sign that someone
has temporarily forgotten that it's
never too late to change their thoughts
and, therefore, their "things."

The Universe

© www.tut.com

FEBRUARY
FEBRERO
FEVRIER

19

Raise your sights and broaden your steps.
Because doing one without the other
is the same as doing neither.

The Universe

© www.tut.com

NOVEMBER
NOVIEMBRE
NOVEMBRE 12

You didn't have to learn how
to make gravity work, did you?
You just had to learn to deal with it.

Same for "thoughts becoming things."

You're already a black belt.

Visualize -
The Universe

© www.tut.com

FEBRUARY
FEBRERO
FEVRIER 20

I have it on good account that you will
soon be called a number of unsavory names...

Lucky, blessed, chosen, gifted, destined, favored,
special, and perhaps, most outrageously,
"not like the rest of us."

Let's give them something to talk about.

The Universe

© www.tut.com

NOVEMBER
NOVIEMBRE
NOVEMBRE 11

The more you "enjoy,"
the richer you become.

Anything, and in every way.

Eureka!
The Universe

© www.tut.com

FEBRUARY
FEBRERO
FEVRIER 21

Good looks have little to do with one's body
and everything to do with one's mind.

Here's looking at you -
The Universe

It also helps to get enough sleep.

© www.tut.com

NOVEMBER
NOVIEMBRE
NOVEMBRE 10

Is it so important that those in your life
fully appreciate how much you mean to them?
Or can you get along just fine knowing it for yourself?

Yeah...

The Universe

Actually, you may even send them right over the edge
if you can truly accept their meager offerings.

© www.tut.com

FEBRUARY
FEBRERO
FEVRIER
22

The absolute, most sure-fire way
of physically moving in the direction of
your dreams, on a day-to-day basis,
without messing with the "cursed hows,"
is living them, now, to any degree that you can.

And you can.

The Universe

© www.tut.com

NOVEMBER
NOVIEMBRE
NOVEMBRE

9

It's up to you.

It's entirely up to you.

And this just might be all you ever have to know.

The Universe

© www.tut.com

FEBRUARY
FEBRERO
FEVRIER **23**

If you can just remember
where this is all going,
no road will be too bumpy,
no night will be too lonely,
and no price will seem too great.

Plus, with just a wink, your confidence
could bring peace to babes and nations.

The Universe

© www.tut.com

NOVEMBER
NOVIEMBRE
NOVEMBRE

8

Kindness always wins.

Always, always, always.

The Universe

Just look at where it's gotten me.

© www.tut.com

An important reason we want to see
your present dreams come true as quickly as
possible is because we already know a little bit
about what will likely happen just beyond them.

Hubba, hubba -
The Universe

© www.tut.com

NOVEMBER
NOVIEMBRE
NOVEMBRE

7

Eternity is a really, really, really long time.

I think we'll be able to squeeze everything in.

Relax.

Peace and blue jeans -
The Universe

© www.tut.com

FEBRUARY
FEBRERO
FEVRIER 25

Sometimes, when a tiny series
of the most unpredictable events occur
that otherwise make no sense at all...
it's just my way of winking and hinting
that something big is about to happen.

The Universe

© www.tut.com

NOVEMBER
NOVIEMBRE
NOVEMBRE
6

Sometimes not knowing what you want
is enough to go on.

After you,
The Universe

Sure beats waiting around for an epiphany, huh?

© www.tut.com

FEBRUARY
FEBRERO
FEVRIER 26

Thinking small isn't easy or hard.
It's just a habit. A habit with consequences.

Same for thinking big.

There is no mountain too great, no sea too wide,
no party too crowded, and no bank account
too fat that you can't take 'em in stride.

The Universe

© www.tut.com

NOVEMBER
NOVIEMBRE
NOVEMBRE

5

Trusting that which you cannot touch,
taste, hear, smell, or see is ultimately how
you'll touch, taste, hear, smell, and see the most.

And we're talkin' all that glitters, giggles,
and gallops, for starters...

Giddy-up,
The Universe

© www.tut.com

FEBRUARY
FEBRERO
FEVRIER

27

In your divinely sanctioned quest
for having, doing, and being ever more,
should you ever need a little inspiration,
simply think of all you now have,
all you now do, and all you now are.

Blows our minds.

The Universe

© www.tut.com

You can always ask yourself
what the "wisest you" would do.

And prepare to be astounded.

Clearly,
The Universe

Just don't answer back out loud
or you may raise a few eyebrows.

© www.tut.com

FEBRUARY
FEBRERO
FEVRIER 28

Have you ever wondered why trees
are such a happy lot?

They've mastered patience.

Either that or it's the music they listen to.

The Universe

© www.tut.com

NOVEMBER
NOVIEMBRE
NOVEMBRE

3

Happily, the distance between having it all,
and not, is only as great as you think.

The Universe

© www.tut.com

FEBRUARY
FEBRERO
FEVRIER 29

(FOR LEAP YEAR)

When the external begins to define
the internal, instead of the internal
defining the external, one begins living
as a mortal rather than as a god.

Trust me, as a god is better.

Boom,
The Universe

© www.tut.com

NOVEMBER
NOVIEMBRE
NOVEMBRE

2

Life's magic is a lot like a swift flowing river.
No matter how long you've overlooked it
or unwittingly swam against it, the instant
you stop struggling you're back in the flow,
hat down low, coolest cat on the block.

The Universe

© www.tut.com

MARCH
MARZO
MARS

1

It's not that folks act a certain way around you,
but rather that you attract certain types of folks
based upon your thoughts, beliefs, and expectations.

Now that is really, really good news, huh?

The Universe

© www.tut.com

NOVEMBER
NOVIEMBRE
NOVEMBRE

1

There's at least one in every crowd...

Someone who's there, first and foremost,
to love you.

Besides me,
The Universe

Good thing I network, huh?

© www.tut.com

MARCH
MARZO
MARS 2

Can you imagine living in a world
where paying too much, giving too much,
and trusting too much would all
inevitably make you more?

Yeah, everything makes you more in time
and space. Especially spending, giving,
and trusting in excess.

The Universe

© www.tut.com

OCTOBER
OCTUBRE
OCTOBRE
31

It's not knowing what the answer
or solution is, but simply knowing that there is one,
which brings it forth.

Of course, you knew that -
The Universe

© www.tut.com

MARCH
MARZO
MARS

3

It's funny, when one links job satisfaction
to financial compensation alone, they're never paid
"enough." Yet, when they see work as a way
to dance with life, meet new people,
and unleash the creative tiger within,
they become very rich, indeed.

The Universe

© www.tut.com

OCTOBER
OCTUBRE
OCTOBRE 30

Once you're prepared, truly prepared
to carry on for as long as it takes, you'll quickly find,
as all movers and shakers have before you,
that it doesn't take long at all.

Surrender to the path, and go -
The Universe

© www.tut.com

MARCH
MARZO
MARS
4

Hey, what if, instead of waiting for everything
to be perfect, we start living your dreams
this week, to any degree that we can?

Ooh-ooh-ooh!
The Universe

Can we start today? Just a little?

© www.tut.com

OCTOBER
OCTUBRE
OCTOBRE 29

Have you noticed how all your life
I've been using you to help make other people's
dreams come true?

Cool. Just didn't want you to think
I haven't noticed it too.

Talk about karma -
The Universe

© www.tut.com

MARCH
MARZO
MARS

5

Often, the very most spiritual thing
one can do is get busy. Physically busy.
Hoeing, chopping, planting.
Connecting, moving, grooving.
Dipping, swirling, twirling.

2, 3, 4 -
The Universe

Yes, "hoeing" is a word.

© www.tut.com

OCTOBER
OCTUBRE
OCTOBRE 28

Nifty, isn't it,
how in life you don't even have to know
how you got where you are,
in order to get where you want to go.

Think, think, and let go -
The Universe

And then, live your little heart out.

© www.tut.com

MARCH
MARZO
MARS

6

Sometimes, far more can be learned
from the disagreeable, than the agreeable.

But I'd still seek out both.

Don't you agree?

The Universe

© www.tut.com

OCTOBER
OCTUBRE
OCTOBRE 27

One of the things I've learned from witnessing
civilization after civilization after civilization
is that one should never underestimate
the profound resiliency of the human spirit,
nor how swiftly things can change for the better,
often overnight.

The Universe

© www.tut.com

MARCH
MARZO
MARS

7

Should you ever hear that voice inside
exclaim that you're working too slow,
are too easily distracted,
or that you should take life more seriously,
please rest assured that it absolutely,
positively, is *not* me.

The Universe

© www.tut.com

OCTOBER
OCTUBRE
OCTOBRE **26**

Oh sure, there will be imposters,
those who make outlandish claims,
and some who are even quite "good,"
but no one, ever, will be another you.

Talk about an advantage,
The Universe

© www.tut.com

MARCH
MARZO
MARS

8

For times when the world seems to spin too fast
or when your dreams seem to turn slightly pale...
switch tracks, give yourself a rest, and dwell
upon the fact that you're still part of a greater
dream. My own. And I couldn't be happier
with the progress we're making.

The Universe

© www.tut.com

OCTOBER
OCTUBRE
OCTOBRE 25

It's funny, the more proficient one becomes
at navigating the ship of their dreams,
the more they leave the navigating to me...
and the smoother the sailing.

And vice versa.

Your nautical wheeler -
The Universe

© www.tut.com

MARCH
MARZO
MARS

9

The more one hurries,
the less time they have.

The Universe

Got that from an accelerated
learning course I once took.

© www.tut.com

OCTOBER
OCTUBRE
OCTOBRE 24

Always, it's the one in motion,
with something to do,
whether humble or grand,
who's the epitome of gorgeous.

Shake, shake, shake…
The Universe

© www.tut.com

MARCH
MARZO
MARS 10

If you could live this life over, would you
still want there to be the same challenges?

Loaded question, huh?

Yeah, you cherry-picked each and every one.
And you knew exactly what you were doing.

In awe of you -
The Universe

© www.tut.com

OCTOBER
OCTUBRE
OCTOBRE

23

Simply imagine happiness,
your own happiness. Feel the smile stretching
across your face, notice the lightness in your step,
hear the sparkle in your voice, and all things,
material and spiritual, will soon fall into place.

The Universe

I am always there.
I am always helping.
I never leave you.
I was there yesterday.
And every day before that.

And I'll be there every day that ever follows.

I mean, where else am I going?

The Universe

© www.tut.com

OCTOBER
OCTUBRE
OCTOBRE
22

The more you find good in another,
the more you'll find good in yourself.

No matter whom that "other" is.

The Universe

© www.tut.com

MARCH
MARZO
MARS
12

Of all your lives, do you know which ones
you'll look back on with the fondest memories,
the most pride, and the widest grin?

The ones where in spite of challenges,
no matter how daunting, difficult, or painful,
you pressed on.

The Universe

© www.tut.com

OCTOBER
OCTUBRE
OCTOBRE **21**

Ironically, those who label others as selfish
are actually more concerned with their own
well-being. And rightly so.

Which simply means, they've yet to see its virtue.

The Universe

© www.tut.com

MARCH
MARZO
MARS 13

Accidents, coincidences, and serendipities
don't create dreams.

Your dreams create them.

Dream away -
The Universe

You can have whatever you want.

© www.tut.com

OCTOBER
OCTUBRE
OCTOBRE
20

Pssssst...

Are you remembering to see the adventure
in every precious moment?

Cool.

Just checking,
The Universe

MARCH
MARZO
MARS 14

Of course, you chose your life.
Your time and place of birth. Your parents.
Your leanings and inclinations.
Hair color. Height. Your savoir-faire.
So that now, on a stage of your own design,
you'd have all you need, to become all you want.

The Universe

© www.tut.com

OCTOBER
OCTUBRE
OCTOBRE 19

It's kind of like your gift to me
is the thoughts you choose,
no matter what you choose.

And my gift to you is their manifestation,
no matter what you think.

Aren't we great?
The Universe

© www.tut.com

MARCH
MARZO
MARS
15

If you knew how each little, fluffy thought
or daydream of yours was tied to the huge,
pivotal events of your life… you'd never again
consider any of your thoughts little or fluffy.

Radical, huh?

The Universe

Good thing we think alike.

© www.tut.com

OCTOBER
OCTUBRE
OCTOBRE 18

You sure can learn a lot about a person
simply from how they say, "Hi" everyday, huh?

And they can learn a lot about you.

The Universe

© www.tut.com

MARCH
MARZO
MARS 16

I do believe it should comfort you to know
that whenever you face a fork in the road of life,
no matter which path you choose,
I'll be there in all my glory.

(Probably moon walking, with a long,
feather boa trailing in the breeze.)

The Universe

© www.tut.com

OCTOBER
OCTUBRE
OCTOBRE 17

You know, if I were you, every time I put on
a garment—a pair of shoes, or gloves, or a t-shirt—
I'd say something really nice to your body.
But that's just me.

I mean, you did kind of "luck out."

The Universe

Oh, go on… nobody can hear you.

© www.tut.com

MARCH
MARZO
MARS 17

Bees can fly 12 miles without getting lost.
Albatrosses, 25,000 miles. And flying insects,
without eyes, have no trouble whatsoever
finding their "soul mates."

Imagine what I can do for you
when you listen to the voice within.

The Universe

Voice, not voices.

© www.tut.com

OCTOBER
OCTUBRE
OCTOBRE 16

Right now, from worlds far away,
as you read these very words,
you're being watched,
every word you speak is being recorded,
and every step you take is being traced.

Talk about fan clubs.

Must be nice,
The Universe

© www.tut.com

MARCH
MARZO
MARS 18

When pondering on the vastness of the cosmos,
please keep in mind that it goes even farther inward
from where you now sit, than outward.

Yeah, you're deep.

The Universe

Save gas, go within - where all of life's mysteries
appear in "primary colors."

© www.tut.com

OCTOBER
OCTUBRE
OCTOBRE
15

Sometimes, when you don't know the answer
to a question that keeps playing over and over again
in your mind, it's because you're messing with the
wrong question.

Do you still love me?
The Universe

© www.tut.com

MARCH
MARZO
MARS 19

In my humble opinion,
the best thing about living in time and space
is having free time.

AND, of course,
remembering that all of your time is free.

Yeah, big AND.

The Universe

© www.tut.com

OCTOBER
OCTUBRE
OCTOBRE
14

Even though you can't physically see
a tree growing, doesn't mean it's not.
Same with the world spinning.

So, next time the masses are huddled at your feet,
pining about dreams they claim aren't coming true,
you might remind them of this.

The Universe

© www.tut.com

MARCH
MARZO
MARS
20

Possessing the audacity to do the mundane
while expecting miracles to come from it,
explains every heroic and supernatural feat
known to humankind.

Audaciously -
The Universe

© www.tut.com

OCTOBER
OCTUBRE
OCTOBRE 13

Once you realize that everything you've ever
been through—every scuffed knee, lost deal,
and broken heart—will eventually play wildly
in your favor, it's kind of hard to complain.

Not that you would anyway.

The Universe

© www.tut.com

MARCH
MARZO
MARS **21**

The things that are common to you,
like windy mornings, starry skies, and old trees;
beetles, strawberries, and doorbells;
coffee, blue jeans, and summertime...
are not common to us.

Enjoy every flippin' moment.

The Universe

© www.tut.com

OCTOBER
OCTUBRE
OCTOBRE 12

How often do you express great and colorful
gratitude for the clarity you now have on your life
and its direction?

Uh-huh...
The Universe

Any color you like.

© www.tut.com

MARCH
MARZO
MARS 22

Permission is what you give yourself.

I give you everything else.

The Universe

There's no need to dally. Your chariot awaits.
Chariots, actually. Your assistant here
insisted you'd want one for every day
of the week. *Assistants*, actually.

© www.tut.com

OCTOBER
OCTUBRE
OCTOBRE
11

Most think that perception works
a lot like a flashlight in the dark,
illuminating whatever it's aimed at.

The truth is, however, that instead of
revealing what's there, it creates it.

The Universe

© www.tut.com

MARCH
MARZO
MARS 23

Don't you just love
super, fabulously wealthy people???

They're exactly like everyone else.

Oh, the glory...
The Universe

What one has done, all can do.

© www.tut.com

OCTOBER
OCTUBRE
OCTOBRE 10

I know this may come as somewhat of a shock,
but of your innumerable and extraordinary gifts,
one day you'll consider your present day
challenges as the greatest of them all.

Trust me.

The Universe

© www.tut.com

MARCH
MARZO
MARS **24**

Do you ever just burst out laughing
when you suddenly remember
that I'm always with you, right by your side,
marshalling the troops, summoning legions,
moving mountains, constantly planning
for the best of times?

The very, very best of times.

The Universe

© www.tut.com

OCTOBER
OCTUBRE
OCTOBRE

9

It was perhaps one of your greatest acts of love.
Choosing to be alive at a time when so many
are so deeply in the dark.

And already things are looking brighter.

All bow,
The Universe

© www.tut.com

MARCH
MARZO
MARS 25

The long and short of it
goes something like this...

When one stops looking for the quick
and easy way, and just deals with what's already
on their plate, the quick and easy way
soon finds them.

Amen,
The Universe

© www.tut.com

OCTOBER
OCTUBRE
OCTOBRE

8

In case anyone should ask,
your heart isn't so large because of your wings;
it's your wings that are so large because of your heart.

Sometimes "loving so much" can be pretty heavy.

Thanks for all you've shared.

The Universe

© www.tut.com

MARCH
MARZO
MARS 26

Every day is a good day
to do something you've never done before.

Especially when you dream of living,
like you've never lived before.

Prepare thy way,
The Universe

Coffee through a straw isn't quite what I meant.

© www.tut.com

OCTOBER
OCTUBRE
OCTOBRE

7

If they hide their power, feign their innocence,
and generally fret that their confidence will rub
some folks the wrong way, it's no wonder
misguided young souls will try to
walk all over them.

Be proud of your magnificence.

The Universe

© www.tut.com

MARCH
MARZO
MARS 27

Don't you just love all those crazy little quarks,
atoms, and molecules that unceasingly manifest
themselves into whatever you're thinking,
no matter how big and daunting,
small and simple, rich and gorgeous?

Just look at 'em all right now.

The Universe

© www.tut.com

OCTOBER
OCTUBRE
OCTOBRE

6

Sometimes the hard way is really the easy way,
and the slow way is really the fast way.

Yet such sublime surprises may remain forever
unknown when one waits... and waits…
for the quick and easy way to manifest.

The Universe

© www.tut.com

MARCH
MARZO
MARS 28

Did you know, the average person looks 793.7%
more attractive when they smile? Not to mention
healthier, wiser, slimmer, richer, and cooler.

They do.

And smiles "become things" too -
The Universe

© www.tut.com

OCTOBER
OCTUBRE
OCTOBRE 5

It's true, the early bird gets the worm.

So does the late bird and the bird in-between. Because, by design, there are always more than enough worms.

In fact, the only bird that doesn't get a worm is the bird that doesn't go out to get one.

Oh, to be alive...
The Universe

© www.tut.com

MARCH
MARZO
MARS 29

You really don't have to try so hard.
That's why there's magic and miracles.
Remember?

You do expect them, right?
Every day, all the time, indoors and out?

The Universe

© www.tut.com

OCTOBER
OCTUBRE
OCTOBRE

4

In case you were wondering, right now,
in the unseen, all bets are on your continued
inevitable success.

Insider trading is legal here.

The Universe

All's fair in love and dreams, especially yours.

© www.tut.com

MARCH
MARZO
MARS **30**

When it comes to the words you choose,
whether in your mind or amongst friends,
let them be of what you like and love.
What you care about and cherish.
What makes you happy. What gives you wings.
What makes you dream. And very little else.

The Universe

© www.tut.com

OCTOBER
OCTUBRE
OCTOBRE

3

Big ideas
almost never seem like big ideas, at first.

So, be on the lookout for little ideas
that seem kind of ho-hum, ain't no big thang,
let me floss first kind of ideas.

Really.

The Universe

© www.tut.com

MARCH
MARZO
MARS 31

It's not as if the currents of life
must be studied, examined, charted, explained, plied,
or channeled in order to be effortlessly ridden upon.
Besides, you'd get soaked.

Let it be easy. You already know
what you need to know, to have it all.

The Universe

© www.tut.com

OCTOBER
OCTUBRE
OCTOBRE

2

It's only after umpteen lifetimes,
a dramatic ascension into peak vibrational levels
of light and awareness, and only after "the way"
has been meticulously prepared and tests have
been passed that a soul can even *hope*
for the kind of life you're now living.

The Universe

© www.tut.com

APRIL
ABRIL
AVRIL
1

By embracing uncertainty
with regard to the "hows" of dream manifestation,
and allowing it, not fearing it, you actually increase
my options for blowing your dear, sweet mind.

Yeah, this is good. Really good.

The Universe

© www.tut.com

OCTOBER
OCTUBRE
OCTOBRE

1

The reason others think they need you
is because they don't yet fully believe
they already have all that it takes
to have all that they want.
So they pretend you hold the key.

And vice versa.

The Universe

© www.tut.com

APRIL
ABRIL
AVRIL
2

This is just your friendly, annual reminder
that things can change so very, very fast.

Passport up to date? Shot card?
Bank deposit slips in your possession at all times?

You're gonna love this year!

The Universe

© www.tut.com

SEPTEMBER
SEPTIEMBRE
SEPTEMBRE 30

It may seem a bit backwards for some,
but the first step one might take towards
rearranging the present circumstances of
their life is to stop dwelling upon the
present circumstances of their life.

But for you it's probably a no-brainer.

The Universe

© www.tut.com

APRIL
ABRIL
AVRIL
3

The reason most people don't recognize
the miracles that are performed on their behalf
is because there's just so bloomin' many of them.

Like this very moment...
And this one...
And this one...

The Universe

© www.tut.com

SEPTEMBER
SEPTIEMBRE
SEPTEMBRE **29**

Freedom from the past,
or anything else for that matter,
always comes in the very instant
you stop thinking about it.

Not that you needed to hear that...
The Universe

© www.tut.com

APRIL
ABRIL
AVRIL

4

No one is ever at the mercy of their past
any more than they're at the mercy of old,
family photo albums.

Just "take more pictures."

The Universe

© www.tut.com

SEPTEMBER
SEPTIEMBRE
SEPTEMBRE
28

Whenever a new disagreement emerges,
so does new hope for enlightenment,
on both sides of the fence.

Oh joy,
The Universe

© www.tut.com

APRIL
ABRIL
AVRIL
5

The more you trust folks,
the less they let you down.

Sounds like an oxymoron, but it's true.

The Universe

Believe me, had you not been as trusting as you already are, there's no telling what some of those rascals would have been up to by now.

© www.tut.com

SEPTEMBER
SEPTIEMBRE
SEPTEMBRE
27

What if every unexpected delay,
postponement, or redirect only meant that at the very
last second, right before the scheduled manifestation,
I had an even better idea?

It happens.

The Universe

© www.tut.com

APRIL
ABRIL
AVRIL
6

The litmus test that will reveal whether or not
those in your company are truly enlightened
is whether or not they treat everyone else
as if they, too, are enlightened.

Best to assume they are, if you get my drift.

All bow,
The Universe

© www.tut.com

SEPTEMBER
SEPTIEMBRE
SEPTEMBRE 26

It's true, sometimes,
when you've had a difficult day,
or met difficult people, or been let down,
disappointed, or heartbroken,
it's easy to completely forget the
most important thing of all...
You're alive.

The Universe

© www.tut.com

APRIL
ABRIL
AVRIL

7

As far as I can tell, worrying about anything
at all is a pretty good indicator that one has begun
thinking that their joy and prosperity
will somehow hinge on pending physical events,
other people, or angry green Martians.

Can you imagine?!

The Universe

© www.tut.com

SEPTEMBER
SEPTIEMBRE
SEPTEMBRE
25

When just starting out on a new journey,
it's only natural to feel vulnerable.
It may seem that you have much to lose.
But may I remind you that never again,
at any other point in the same journey,
will you have so much to gain?

The Universe

© www.tut.com

APRIL
ABRIL
AVRIL

8

Impatience is a sign

that one has temporarily forgotten to behave,
at all times, as if their dreams have already
come true.

You know, in case someone asks.

The Universe

© www.tut.com

SEPTEMBER
SEPTIEMBRE
SEPTEMBRE
24

Often, having what you want
is a function of letting go
of what you have.

If you know what I mean.

The Universe

Odd, huh, the stuff people cling to?

© www.tut.com

APRIL
ABRIL
AVRIL
9

Did you know that if you choose to be joyful
enough, it's physically impossible to get angry,
fret, stew, or worry?

And if you choose it often enough, it's physically
impossible to be broke, sick, lonely, or confused?

Some things really are impossible.

The Universe

© www.tut.com

SEPTEMBER
SEPTIEMBRE
SEPTEMBRE 23

If you only gave yourself credit
for all the things you do that you don't
give yourself credit for,
you'd be astonished to learn how much
you really do accomplish in a single day.
Every single day.

The Universe

© www.tut.com

APRIL
ABRIL
AVRIL 10

Perhaps the very best thing that happens
to souls who are suddenly overwhelmed by torrents
of financial abundance is that they start working
simply for the fun of it.

Hey! You can already do that!

"Work," it's not just for the wealthy anymore.

The Universe

© www.tut.com

SEPTEMBER
SEPTIEMBRE
SEPTEMBRE 22

I hope you know how important you are
in contributing to the "all things are exactly
as they should be" concept, on this very day.

Because without you, they wouldn't be.

The Universe

© www.tut.com

APRIL
ABRIL
AVRIL

11

Judging yourself
for what you haven't yet accomplished
is kind of like taking rocket fuel from a rocket
so that it might fly higher.

I said, "kind of."

The Universe

The rocket needs fuel…
and you deserve a standing ovation.

© www.tut.com

The subtle secret
to possessing all you want:
Blessing all you have.

Haiku. Haiku very much. Haiku.

The Universe

© www.tut.com

APRIL
ABRIL
AVRIL
12

Wild, isn't it, how the physical manifestations
and experiences of your life hinge so much
on your daydreams.

Dreaming of you,
The Universe

© www.tut.com

SEPTEMBER
SEPTIEMBRE
SEPTEMBRE 20

What most mortals don't quite realize
is that for every thought they think,
the physical world is instantly changed.

But then, that's what makes them mortal.

Oh, the places you will go -
The Universe

© www.tut.com

APRIL
ABRIL
AVRIL
13

There are indeed times in every life
when one must simply lay low, hide out, and chill.

And usually it's called sleep.

However, in-between such times, by the light of
the sun or a giant disco ball, I generally advocate
as full a schedule as you can possibly manage.

The Universe

© www.tut.com

**SEPTEMBER
SEPTIEMBRE
SEPTEMBRE** 19

Do you know how most people get jobs
they love? They first loved the job they had,
and everyone noticed. And do I mean everyone.

The same goes for people with cars they love,
homes they love, people they love,
and bodies they love.

The Universe

© www.tut.com

I just had this crazy experience!
I was riding my bike to the beach
(I do stuff like that, you know)
and for just a moment, completely forgot
that I was the whole, entire Universe...

Does that ever happen to you?

The Universe

© www.tut.com

SEPTEMBER
SEPTIEMBRE
SEPTEMBRE

18

What if I told you that your every conflict,
disappointment, struggle, or challenge with others
and yourself, was merely a manifestation
of what's going on within your own thinking.
Would you go there first to fix, mend, and allay?

The Universe

© www.tut.com

APRIL
ABRIL
AVRIL **15**

Don't let the dazzling heights you aspire to
scare you from getting started.

After all, few could climb Mt. Everest tomorrow,
though virtually all could begin preparing.

The Universe

© www.tut.com

SEPTEMBER
SEPTIEMBRE
SEPTEMBRE
17

An end result,
imagined clearly and acted upon with expectation,
will always force the circumstances necessary
to bring about its own manifestation,
no matter how unpredictable, unlikely,
or even "impossible" those circumstances
may have previously seemed.

The Universe

© www.tut.com

APRIL
ABRIL
AVRIL 16

If you hold it clearly enough in mind;
if you physically anticipate it, steadily, day by day,
there are no earthly hands, nor heavenly
for that matter, which can halt its subsequent
manifestation into your life.

Just be really, really sure you want it.

The Universe

© www.tut.com

SEPTEMBER
SEPTIEMBRE
SEPTEMBRE 16

When you see things that pain you,
that sadden you, or that make your heart ache,
remember... you're not seeing all.

I hope you never need this one.

All love,
The Universe

© www.tut.com

The difference between how you
sometimes see yourself and how I see you,
could be summed up like this:

You wonder, at times, what it is you might do
that you'd be wildly successful at.
And I wonder, at times, how you
seem to miss that you already are.

The Universe

© www.tut.com

SEPTEMBER
SEPTIEMBRE
SEPTEMBRE 15

While you might, from time to time,
envy others, it's precisely during those moments
when you might ask yourself whether or not
you'd actually like to be them.

Envy cured, huh?

The Universe

© www.tut.com

APRIL
ABRIL
AVRIL
18

Apologize to an old soul
and your gesture will be honored.
Apologize to a young soul
and matters may become extremely complicated.

Apologize anyway.

The Universe

Happily, hanging around afterwards is purely optional.

© www.tut.com

SEPTEMBER
SEPTIEMBRE
SEPTEMBRE

14

Since you're in a position to help so many,
please remind them, when necessary,
that setbacks are only ever devastating
when one thinks they'll last forever.

They never do.

The Universe

© www.tut.com

APRIL
ABRIL
AVRIL **19**

An old soul is always prepared to admit
they might be wrong, especially when they're not.

I think.

Older than the moon,
The Universe

© www.tut.com

SEPTEMBER
SEPTIEMBRE
SEPTEMBRE 13

You have only to smile
and the choirs here become absolutely deafening.

Sometimes even a half-raised eyebrow will do it.

Your #1 fan,
The Universe

© www.tut.com

APRIL
ABRIL
AVRIL 20

Not everyone can say they're all powerful,
eternal, loved beyond imagination,
and followed around by hordes of angels.

Well... yeah, actually, they can.

But the point is, do you?

The Universe

© www.tut.com

SEPTEMBER
SEPTIEMBRE
SEPTEMBRE
12

Haven't you noticed?

The right people always find each other
at the right time.

Relax,
The Universe

© www.tut.com

APRIL
ABRIL
AVRIL
21

Did you know that if you can see a cloud,
it can see you?

Same for trees.

And beauty.

Kind of makes you want to go out more, huh?

The Universe

© www.tut.com

SEPTEMBER
SEPTIEMBRE
SEPTEMBRE

11

Sometimes, the one person
who you think can help you the least,
can help you the most.

Galling, isn't it?

The Universe

© www.tut.com

APRIL
ABRIL
AVRIL 22

9 out of 10 old souls agree
that one of the very best things about spiritual maturity,
besides the discounts, is appreciating that age is so
very meaningless.

The 10th soul? Presently out climbing trees
and could not be reached.

The Universe

© www.tut.com

SEPTEMBER
SEPTIEMBRE
SEPTEMBRE 10

A super secret money insight,
from your magician friend, The Universe...

While great joy inevitably yields great abundance,
rarely does this relationship work in reverse.

Dream of "the life," not the money.

The Universe

© www.tut.com

APRIL
ABRIL
AVRIL 23

It's as if everyone has a built-in, happiness-now
button, which can instantly change how they feel,
no matter what's going on in their lives.

But for many, most of the time,
they prefer not to push it.

Go on, push it real good -
The Universe

© www.tut.com

SEPTEMBER
SEPTIEMBRE
SEPTEMBRE

9

While it's often fashionable to dwell upon
what might have been, what's usually overlooked
is that, really and truly, it couldn't have.

Because, invariably, any romanticized versions
of how things "might have been," are based upon
fictionalized versions of the past.

The Universe

© www.tut.com

APRIL
ABRIL
AVRIL 24

Whenever an escalator to "success" ascends
without you (just "swoosh-h-h-h-h!" right into
the sky leaving you stuck on the ground),
it's always because there's another one
on the way that will go even higher,
with your name plastered all over it.

The Universe

SEPTEMBER
SEPTIEMBRE
SEPTEMBRE

8

The great perfection lies in the fact
that no matter what happens next,
you'll be richer for it.

Much richer.

The Universe

© www.tut.com

APRIL
ABRIL
AVRIL **25**

The trick is remembering that at all times
far more is happening on your behalf
than your physical senses will ever reveal.

Like right now.

The Universe

© www.tut.com

SEPTEMBER
SEPTIEMBRE
SEPTEMBRE

7

One way to defeat invisible, limiting beliefs,
even ones you may not know you have,
is to simply dream of a life so grand
that they couldn't possibly make sense.
And then start living that life today,
however humbly at first.

The Universe

© www.tut.com

APRIL
ABRIL
AVRIL **26**

If one stopped thinking about what others
thought, said, and did, hardly anything
would ever bother them again.

At least that's what I think -
The Universe

© www.tut.com

SEPTEMBER
SEPTIEMBRE
SEPTEMBRE

6

It's really, really simple.
Love what you do (what you're now doing),
and you'll become a magnet for all things good.

As if you needed the extra incentive.

The Universe

© www.tut.com

APRIL
ABRIL
AVRIL
27

You know, it's totally possible to have big,
huge, gigantic dreams, yet still be deliriously happy
with today.

I call it the built-in double-happiness
redundancy factor.

The Universe

© www.tut.com

SEPTEMBER
SEPTIEMBRE
SEPTEMBRE

5

If you really think about it,
you can always know what's going to happen next:
I'm going to be there. I'm going to help.
And there will be miracles.

The Universe

And there will be those who wonder
where you've been all their life.

© www.tut.com

APRIL
ABRIL
AVRIL
28

Don't worry that some seem not to notice
your refinement, enlightenment, and sashay.
They're still learning from you in their own way.

No matter what they say or don't say, they chose
to know you because it would make them more.

The Universe

© www.tut.com

SEPTEMBER
SEPTIEMBRE
SEPTEMBRE

4

The odd thing about inspiration

is that it often comes after, not before,
a new journey is started.

The Universe

So go on, break the ice! Put on that tutu,
spin a whirly, clutch the sky, and you'll have them
quivering in their boots in no time at all...
or am I thinking of someone else?

© www.tut.com

APRIL
ABRIL
AVRIL 29

Do you think most realize
that what they're really after is more "living,"
not more rewards? Yet by conditioning the former
upon the latter, they have a tough time with both?

Yeah, not yet. But one day they will.

The Universe

© www.tut.com

SEPTEMBER
SEPTIEMBRE
SEPTEMBRE

3

Next time you overhear someone say
they're only human, be compassionate.

But remind them it's only temporary.
That before long, they'll be able to see their
wings again, speak in tongues, and blaze trails
through eternity upon chariots of fire.

The Universe

© www.tut.com

APRIL
ABRIL
AVRIL 30

The trick with spending money
lies in knowing, with every fiber of your being,
that it will return.

And so it must.

As if on wings -
The Universe

© www.tut.com

SEPTEMBER
SEPTIEMBRE
SEPTEMBRE

2

The banquet's been prepared,
the guests are all gathered, and excitement fills the air...

This is how we begin every morning,
watching you rise from bed.

The Universe

It's one big party. Every day there are miracles.
And you're never alone.

© www.tut.com

MAY
MAYO
MAI

1

Rarely, are the first steps in a journey
anything like the final ones,
either in direction, pace, or grace.
So please believe me when I tell you
that none of those things are even half as
important as is that there are steps at all.

The Universe

© www.tut.com

SEPTEMBER
SEPTIEMBRE
SEPTEMBRE

1

Fortunately, disappointments have little
to do with circumstance and everything
to do with perspective.

Everything.

The Universe

© www.tut.com

MAY
MAYO
MAI
2

Do you think for a single instant,
I'd have ever "let you go" if all the lions, and tigers,
and bears weren't illusion, and all the friends,
laughter, and happy times weren't real?

Well do you?

Silly...
The Universe

© www.tut.com

AUGUST
AGOSTO
AOÛT **31**

No one really cares about your "stuff,"
if you don't care about your "stuff."

They're far more interested in their own "stuff."

The Universe

Let's really give them something to talk about.

© www.tut.com

MAY
MAYO
MAI

3

Sometimes, when things take longer
than you thought they would, it's just a gentle
reminder from your greater Self (me),
that you have more time than you thought,
and that there's a journey to enjoy.

The Universe

© www.tut.com

AUGUST
AGOSTO
AOÛT
30

You know that dreamy look of deep,
soulful love you've sometimes seen in the eyes
of another as they gazed into your own?

Expect a lot more of it.

The Universe

© www.tut.com

MAY
MAYO
MAI

4

Love, truth, and enlightenment.
The door, the key, and the inevitable.

In case you were wondering.

The Universe

© www.tut.com

AUGUST
AGOSTO
AOÛT
29

In a slightly different world, if dogs believed
in "soul mates" when it came to choosing their owners,
can you imagine how lonesome most would be?

Oh, there's definitely room for "picky,"
but there's also room for "surprise me."

Surprise me,
The Universe

© www.tut.com

MAY
MAYO
MAI
5

While one's capacity to dream great dreams
is truly infinite, the capacity to do great things
is mightily dependent upon one's ability to do
little, baby, trite, mortal, dull,
and sometimes silly things.

The Universe

© www.tut.com

All pain is self-inflicted.

Ouch...
The Universe

Which, quite frankly, is fantastic news,
since it means you needn't feel it anymore.

© www.tut.com

MAY
MAYO
MAI

6

In time and space, if you just look for
what's right—in others, in relationships, in yourself,
and in your journey—you'll always find it.

Same when looking for what's wrong.

The Universe

Now that's perfection.

© www.tut.com

AUGUST
AGOSTO
AOÛT 27

If you can fall in love with one thing
about him, her, them, it, or yourself,
just once a day, and speak it aloud,
you'll be surprised by how quickly
it will transform your entire life.

I love that look on your face when the coin drops -
The Universe

© www.tut.com

MAY
MAYO
MAI

7

You can always tell a master
by the kindness in their eyes.

And yours look lovely today.

The Universe

Oh yeah, and they're usually
the last to know that they're masters.

© www.tut.com

AUGUST
AGOSTO
AOÛT 26

The hardest thing for most to understand
about manifesting major life changes is that
it's so easy.

Child's play -
The Universe

It was never meant to be hard.
You're a creator. You can have anything.

© www.tut.com

MAY
MAYO
MAI
8

Do you want to know why I have an issue
with compromising, economizing, and settling for less?

I have to work just as hard whether the bar
has been lowered or raised.

The Universe

Dream even BIGGER.

© www.tut.com

AUGUST
AGOSTO
AOÛT
25

There's a reason you chose Earth,
exactly when you did, as exactly who you are,
with those already in your life and those who soon will be:
To be an example, to shine your light, and to give hope.

Yeah, you were needed... super bad.

The Universe

© www.tut.com

MAY
MAYO
MAI
9

The trick is learning to maintain
an unwavering focus upon your desired end result,
your completed dream, the "finish line,"
without insisting upon or contemplating its means
of attainment, no matter how logical, obvious,
or tempting it may seem.

The Universe

© www.tut.com

AUGUST
AGOSTO
AOÛT 24

Almost no one ever says it will be easy.

Actually, most say it will be hard.
Really, really hard.

What do you tell yourself, day after day?

The Universe

Besides all the sweet talk.

© www.tut.com

MAY
MAYO
MAI 10

Don't fret; wanting "more"
is just the first sign of many
that you're going to get it.

How cool is that?

The Universe

© www.tut.com

AUGUST
AGOSTO
AOÛT

23

Dang, just because you're a supernatural,
unstoppable, manifesting machine,
doesn't mean you can't ask for help.
A lot of help. And fully expect to receive it.

That was part of "the deal" -
The Universe

© www.tut.com

MAY
MAYO
MAI

11

It only takes one idea, one second in time,
one friend, one dream, one leap of faith,
to change everything, forever.

Just one!

Yet eternity lies in the palm of your hand.

Hallelujah,
The Universe

© www.tut.com

AUGUST
AGOSTO
AOÛT
22

Little tiny dreams require little tiny thoughts
and little tiny steps.

Great big dreams require great big thoughts
and little tiny steps.

Do I paint a clear picture?
The Universe

© www.tut.com

MAY
MAYO
MAI

12

Always trust your dreams.

They've chosen you, as much as you've
chosen them.

The Universe

© www.tut.com

AUGUST
AGOSTO
AOÛT 21

A mirror never lies, and neither does time
or space as a reflection of what you're thinking.
If you put it out there, it has to come back.
No matter how much it weighs, glitters, or costs.

It's the law.

The Universe

© www.tut.com

MAY
MAYO
MAI
13

Whenever conferring with another
—either face to face or across the miles—
whether a human being, departed spirit, or sentient tree,
always speak to the highest within them.

It makes such a difference.

The Universe

© www.tut.com

AUGUST
AGOSTO
AOÛT
20

Actually, smiling or laughing for no reason at all
is one of the best reasons to smile or laugh.
Because doing either, turns wheels in the unseen,
rearranges players in your life, and summons reason
after reason after reason.

Grins,
The Universe

© www.tut.com

MAY
MAYO
MAI
14

To be beautiful in the eyes of another,
simply forget they're watching.

The Universe

Oh, of course they are...
Now, forget I just told you that.

© www.tut.com

AUGUST
AGOSTO
AOÛT 19

Do you know what happens
when folks distrust the trustworthy?
They begin attracting the untrustworthy.
And for those who trust the untrustworthy?
They begin attracting the trustworthy.

Trust me,
The Universe

Better to trust everyone.

© www.tut.com

MAY
MAYO
MAI
15

If you knew how much you have in common
with every single person now living in time and space,
in terms of your deepest hopes and dreams,
fears and worries, you'd wonder how I manage
to tell you all apart.

The Universe

© www.tut.com

AUGUST
AGOSTO
AOÛT 18

Ten thousand years from now,
your presence will still be felt,
your name will still be whispered,
and your goodness will still be expanding.

And that's just for the stuff you've already done!

You're a supa-star,
The Universe

© www.tut.com

MAY
MAYO
MAI
16

New souls look to secrets, rights, and rituals.

Advanced souls look to science, math, and evidence.

And old souls look within.

Look within,
The Universe

© www.tut.com

AUGUST
AGOSTO
AOÛT

17

Has it occurred to you
that you could ask for more?
Not just more than what you now have,
but more than you're now asking for?

This is why I'm HOT -
The Universe

I would hate to see the look on your face,
learning this after the fact!

© www.tut.com

MAY
MAYO
MAI
17

In case you were wondering
what might happen next, how this week will unfold,
who you will become tomorrow, and so on,
it all boils down to one thing:

Expectation.

Yours.

The Universe

© www.tut.com

AUGUST
AGOSTO
AOÛT
16

Some folks, not having lived perhaps
as much as you, endured as much, or loved as much,
simply cannot see the truth of a situation,
disagreement, or relationship as clearly as you.

And so, it's wise to keep in mind
that it's not their fault.

The Universe

© www.tut.com

MAY
MAYO
MAI 18

In all of time and space,
can you think of anything more
valuable than just another day?

Well, if you can, I'll give that to you as well.

Feeling groovy,
The Universe

How's that for a reality check?

© www.tut.com

AUGUST
AGOSTO
AOÛT
15

Actually, it's not as if your angels can just drop
everything they're doing and come running whenever
you call for assistance, guidance, and love.

You pretty much are everything they're doing.

Before you even ask,
The Universe

© www.tut.com

MAY
MAYO
MAI **19**

When walls close in, skies turn gray,
and dreams seem like they're awfully far away,
you're probably just forgetting that the same "hands"
that created the sun, the moon, and the stars,
are still holding yours, anxious to help.

The Universe

© www.tut.com

AUGUST
AGOSTO
AOÛT 14

The person who remembers
they can always reach out and help others,
never runs out of things to do, always has friends,
and rarely needs advice.

"Give it away, give it away, give it away, give it away now,"
The Universe

They worry less, too.

© www.tut.com

MAY
MAYO
MAI **20**

To find out how much you've truly been blessed
with in terms of love, time, energy, talent, joy,
abundance, confidence, intelligence, wit, or
any other quality, substance, or dispensation,
give of them.

Then you'll know what boundless really means.

The Universe

© www.tut.com

AUGUST
AGOSTO
AOÛT
13

It's always been easy to love you.

The challenge has come from granting
you so much freedom that, at times,
you might not know that I do.

I always have,
The Universe

I always will.

© www.tut.com

MAY
MAYO
MAI
21

Here's what I ask folks who aspire to being
fabulously rich:

"Couldn't you just pretend you're a multi, multi-millionaire?"

"You know, right after you're done pretending you're not."

O-o-o-o-o-o-o-o-o-u-h...
The Universe

It's all "pretend."

© www.tut.com

AUGUST
AGOSTO
AOÛT
12

Do you know who I really, really love?

The folks who keep doing little things,
expecting BIG results, especially when circumstances
seem to indicate that tomorrow will pretty much be
exactly the same as yesterday.

These are the world's movers and shakers.

The Universe

© www.tut.com

MAY
MAYO
MAI
22

When you finally get that call,
meet that person, walk that walk, and live that dream,
do you think you'll even care that there were a few dark
and scary moments in a journey that made them all possible?

Trust me, you won't even remember.

The Universe

© www.tut.com

AUGUST
AGOSTO
AOÛT
11

Have you ever noticed
that there's really only one thing
you can do to unquestionably change
the scenery in your life?

Physically move through it.

In the fast lane,
The Universe

© www.tut.com

MAY
MAYO
MAI 23

When you feel happy, really happy,
it somehow seems that you've always been happy
and that you'll always be happy.

The same is often true when you feel sad, or lonely,
or depressed, or broke, or sick, or scared.

Something, perhaps, to remember.

The Universe

© www.tut.com

AUGUST
AGOSTO
AOÛT
10

The only person
you really have to make happy
is you.

There's no one I trust or believe in more
on such an important subject.

Good thing you're so cool -
The Universe

© www.tut.com

MAY
MAYO
MAI
24

The presumption, at all times
and under all circumstances, should always be that you
are good enough, worthy enough, and lovable enough.
And that you are exactly the right kind of person,
in the right place, at the right time. Otherwise,
you wouldn't have been instilled with such
dreams in the first place.

The Universe

© www.tut.com

AUGUST
AGOSTO
AOÛT

9

Your words are simply the thoughts of yours
that will become things the soonest.

Awesome, huh?

The Universe

Have a wonderfully wordy day.

© www.tut.com

MAY
MAYO
MAI **25**

Of all the wonderful places you'll go,
of all the happy times you'll have,
of all the adventures that now call unto you,
each will be enhanced and will more quickly
come to pass... with your absolute immersion
into today's places, times, and adventures.

The Universe

© www.tut.com

AUGUST
AGOSTO
AOÛT

8

Hey… you're not using all of your angels.
What's up with that?

Use all of your angels.
Run faster, jump higher, get more.

Call, ask, give thanks -
The Universe

Best of all, the more you use, the more you get!

© www.tut.com

MAY
MAYO
MAI

26

If you look closely enough
into the eyes of another,
no matter who they are,
you will always see me.

Go on, try it -
The Universe

© www.tut.com

You can always tell an old soul
by how friendly they are to trees.

Very, very -
The Universe

To dogs, too.

© www.tut.com

Emotional pains are just truth knocking
upon a door that's been closed too long.

Always.

The Universe

Chorus: "Le-e-e-e-e-e-t the sunshine in..."

© www.tut.com

AUGUST
AGOSTO
AOÛT

6

If you sit and get really quiet,
fully expecting your answer,
it has to come.

Guaranteed,
The Universe

Expectation unlocks all doors,
lights all paths, and frosts all cakes.

© www.tut.com

MAY
MAYO
MAI
28

There are no sane reasons to limit a dream.
After all, you don't have to deliver it. I do.

Faithfully,
The Universe

That's right. Go ahead. Raise the bar. Higher.
Higher, still. As if it was me who had to jump it.

© www.tut.com

AUGUST
AGOSTO
AOÛT

5

I do wonder how it is that you don't ALL
just fall crazy in love with each other
and get it over with.

Falling in love, I mean.

I have -
The Universe

© www.tut.com

MAY
MAYO
MAI 29

Show me someone
who keeps getting in your way,
and I'll show you someone
who keeps making excuses.

Tricky, tricky, tricky,
The Universe

© www.tut.com

AUGUST
AGOSTO
AOÛT 4

If there was an event

that was so super-extraordinary, so rare, and
so fantastically incredible that it only happened
once every 7 to 10 billion years, it would still be
infinitely more ordinary, routine, and credible
than the passage of today.

The Universe

© www.tut.com

MAY
MAYO
MAI
30

Happiness always returns.

You know, in case you should ever
sense its absence.

The Universe

Partly, because while it's away, it misses you
even more than you miss it.

© www.tut.com

AUGUST
AGOSTO
AOÛT
3

It's like, the more you give yourself to do,
the more time you're given to do it.

BIG LOVE,
The Universe

© www.tut.com

It's wise never to ask another for what you want.

No, don't ask me.

No, not even yourself.

Just give thanks, in advance. As if you already had whatever it is the "old-you" would have asked for.

The Universe

© www.tut.com

AUGUST
AGOSTO
AOÛT

2

Ever notice that in the long run
those who don't eventually go "within,"
often go "without"?

You've got the power,
The Universe

That's where all the answers lie.

© www.tut.com

JUNE
JUNIO
JUIN

1

The need to criticize simply belies a longing
for recognition, appreciation, and validation.
None of which, however, can be obtained
through criticism.

I'm sure it's just a phase they're going through.

Wink,
The Universe

© www.tut.com

AUGUST
AGOSTO
AOÛT

1

See through the fog that tells others
nothing matters, nothing is happening,
and it does no good.

They realize not that every second of history...
was optional.

Oh the glory, the sublime glory.

The Universe

© www.tut.com

JUNE
JUNIO
JUIN
2

The real reason animals don't talk
is because they understand so much.

Word,
The Universe

Verily, the more understanding one possesses,
the less there is to say, and the more
there is to do.

Baby steps spark miracles.

Miracles do not spark baby steps.

Ungawa,
The Universe

The only miracles that can't reach you
are the ones you wait around for!

JUNE
JUNIO
JUIN
3

Do you know what's really, really, really easy?

Whatever you say is really, really, really easy.

Same goes for the hard stuff.

You so fly,
The Universe

© www.tut.com

JULY
JULIO
JUILLET 30

If it's hard, there's something you're missing.

Give it a little more thought, and remember,
you're not alone, you have "helpers,"
and the entire Universe is on your side...
with insights, guidance, and support
only a whisper away.

The Universe

© www.tut.com

JUNE
JUNIO
JUIN

4

Perhaps the greatest of all illusions
is that life could somehow be better
than it already is.

You've got it made -
The Universe

© www.tut.com

JULY
JULIO
JUILLET 29

Just a friendly reminder...

The shortest distance between here and there,
between have and have not, is always through imagination.
Let yours pave the way by imagining the end result.

Thoughts become things.

They really, really, really do.

The Universe

© www.tut.com

JUNE
JUNIO
JUIN

5

Always remember,
when it comes to climbing mountains,
slaying dragons, or just plain getting what you want,
you've got a built-in, double-secret advantage:
You're supernatural.

Shhhh... don't tell the lesser-mortals.

The Universe

JULY
JULIO
JUILLET
28

There is a purpose, a plan, and a reason
for all things. What doesn't make sense, will make sense.

You are exactly where you should be.
Your challenges are what they should be.
Your rewards are what they should be.
And the best is yet to come.

The Universe

© www.tut.com

JUNE
JUNIO
JUIN

6

Not everyone can say, "I love you."

But they all do.

What a world,
The Universe

© www.tut.com

JULY
JULIO
JUILLET 27

Whether or not you can now see it,
there is always a way.

Let this truth be the guiding light
in all you think, say, and do forever more.

The Universe

© www.tut.com

Healing happens. Non-stop.

There's only healing.

Rest easy -
The Universe

© www.tut.com

JULY
JULIO
JUILLET 26

Don't let those who aren't in tune with you,
distract you from those who are.

Trust.

The Universe

© www.tut.com

JUNE
JUNIO
JUIN

8

Frightened, worried, doubtful?
Sometimes, instead of trying to imagine
the opposite of what you're afraid of,
it's easier to just imagine happiness.

Works just as fast… maybe faster.

The Universe

© www.tut.com

JULY
JULIO
JUILLET 25

This Note requires action.

Why not let today mark the beginning
of the absolute happiest, most memorable
time of your life?

The power is yours. Do something.

The Universe

© www.tut.com

JUNE
JUNIO
JUIN

9

Sometimes, finally seeing things
from someone else's perspective
can totally change your life.

Which, sometimes, explains exactly why they're there.

Spooky,
The Universe

© www.tut.com

JULY
JULIO
JUILLET 24

Pop Quiz!

Q: How do you find love, health, abundance, and enlightenment?

A: Stop searching. And start seeing what has been there all along.

The Universe

© www.tut.com

JUNE
JUNIO
JUIN 10

If you just think what you know to think,
say what you know to say, and do what you know to do,
you'll blow all their little minds.

Cool?

The Universe

And you know exactly what to think, say, and do.

© www.tut.com

JULY
JULIO
JUILLET 23

Ever wonder how many angels you have?

ALL of them.

They insisted.

The Universe

© www.tut.com

JUNE
JUNIO
JUIN
11

Sometimes when a door is slammed shut,
the very best thing you can do is to knock again,
and again, and again.

The Universe

But I'd recommend you try all the other doors, too.

© www.tut.com

JULY
JULIO
JUILLET **22**

On earth, it seems that most people fret,
worry, and lose sleep over some of the silliest things
they've done.

But what's funny is that later on, from here, more often
than not, it's the things they didn't do that haunt them.

The Universe

© www.tut.com

JUNE
JUNIO
JUIN
12

Goodness gracious,
I thought you realized by now...

Nothing has to happen.

This is paradise.

Love, love,
The Universe

© www.tut.com

JULY
JULIO
JUILLET 21

Do you know what the "point" of it all is?

This whole contraption of time and space
was designed and engineered to scientifically prove
that you are endowed with all you need,
to have all you want.

Everything else is just fluff.

The Universe

© www.tut.com

JUNE
JUNIO
JUIN
13

Know what's missing from most people's lives?

The realization that nothing is missing from their lives.

You already have whatever you may be looking for.

The Universe

© www.tut.com

JULY
JULIO
JUILLET 20

Always, the best remedy
for dealing with a troubling past
is living in the present.
Not just "being" in the present
(unless you're a tree),
but "living" in it.

The Universe

© www.tut.com

JUNE
JUNIO
JUIN
14

You're not supposed to be able to see it
with your eyes first. It wouldn't be called "manifesting"
if you could.

See it with your mind first.

That's what it's there for, sort of -
The Universe

© www.tut.com

JULY
JULIO
JUILLET 19

The more you believe in appearances,
in the story told by your physical senses and
in the circumstances that you now find yourself in,
the less control you have over them.

What's real is your power to change them.

The Universe

All things are possible.

© www.tut.com

JUNE
JUNIO
JUIN

15

The secret to always being at the right place,
at the right time, is knowing you always are.

Like today. Like now.

Because you are, and all is well.

The Universe

© www.tut.com

JULY
JULIO
JUILLET 18

If you know what you want;
if you've made up your mind;
if you can see it, feel it, and move towards it
in some small way, every single day...
it has to happen.

xxxooo,

The Universe

© www.tut.com

JUNE
JUNIO
JUIN 16

Until everyone believes in their own ability
to say exactly the right thing, at exactly the right time,
to exactly the right person, then allow me:

Everyone wants to be your friend. Everyone.

You're just cool.

The Universe

And those who are your friends... are tickled pink.

© www.tut.com

JULY
JULIO
JUILLET 17

If you just start dancing,
I can assure you, by the powers vested in me
(more than you could ever imagine),
the music will be added. As will the partners,
the giant disco ball, and whatever else you like.

Do your thing and I'll do mine,
The Universe

© www.tut.com

JUNE
JUNIO
JUIN
17

To clarify "eternal" just a smidge...

Once the river of time has rounded her final bend,
and the last star in the sky has brightened its last night,
and every child who may ever be conceived
has been given ten thousand names...
we will have just begun.

The Universe

© www.tut.com

JULY
JULIO
JUILLET 16

Sometimes, when it seems your wings
have suddenly and unexpectedly been clipped,
maybe, just maybe, there's more to learn
by staying where you are.

The Universe

© www.tut.com

JUNE
JUNIO
JUIN
18

Do you know what the emotional highs
and lows, on any given day, can tell an astute
observer about themselves?

Yep, exactly what they've been telling themselves,
on any given day.

The Universe

Say the good stuff.

© www.tut.com

JULY
JULIO
JUILLET 15

It's one kind of victory to slay a beast,
move a mountain, and cross a chasm,
but it's another kind altogether to realize
that the beast, the mountain, and the chasm
were of your own design.

The Universe

© www.tut.com

JUNE
JUNIO
JUIN **19**

Neither worthiness, effort, skill, intelligence,
talent, timing, connections, looks, popularity,
blood, sweat, or tears will make the difference.

More than anything else, living in wealth
and abundance is simply a matter of knowing
that you already do.

The Universe

© www.tut.com

Whoohoooooo! Guess what?

Everything,
absolutely everything you've ever wanted,
now lies within reach!

Of course... you still have to reach.

The Universe

JUNE
JUNIO
JUIN **20**

Of course, you do see that in your world
of constant change, the only thing that's really changing
is you and what you choose to understand?

Even time and space are simply measurements
of self-awareness.

The Universe

© www.tut.com

JULY
JULIO
JUILLET 13

It's as if when you move, I move.
When you reach, I reach.
And when you go the extra mile, I clear the way.
But not a moment sooner.

Which is why, before you commit,
things can sometimes look so scary.

Just like that,
The Universe

© www.tut.com

JUNE
JUNIO
JUIN 21

Young souls get angry at others.

Old souls get angry at themselves.

But really wise souls have already turned the page.

Got forever and ever?
The Universe

No trifling of the past, no matter how great,
can tarnish the brilliance of eternity.

© www.tut.com

JULY
JULIO
JUILLET 12

When the choice
is to hurt or be hurt.
Cheat or be cheated.
Violate or be violated.

Always, always, always choose the latter.

Trust me,
The Universe

Besides, having such choices are never random.

© www.tut.com

JUNE
JUNIO
JUIN 22

Actually, the only effective way of changing
another person is by changing yourself.

Works every time, guaranteed.

The Universe

Though, I'm kind of partial to the way
you are right now.

© www.tut.com

JULY
JULIO
JUILLET
11

Anger is one of enlightenment's
many barometers.

Basically, the more you have of one,
the less you have of the other.

Yes-sir-ee-bob,
The Universe

Don't get mad, get smart.

© www.tut.com

JUNE
JUNIO
JUIN
23

Ironically, had it not been for every
disappointment, setback, and detour in the road
of your life, you wouldn't have come so far.

Nice strategy.

Love, love,
The Universe

© www.tut.com

JULY
JULIO
JUILLET 10

It totally flips me out. People talk to me,
they ask me stuff, they show me things...
yet so rarely do they ever expect a reply.

Are you feeling me?
The Universe

© www.tut.com

JUNE
JUNIO
JUIN
24

Between here and there,
the only thing that matters is what you think,
from now 'til then.

Choices, choices, choices.

The Universe

The past is simply what you choose to remember,
if you even choose to remember it.

© www.tut.com

JULY
JULIO
JUILLET

9

Would you believe that there are some people
who actually think they can change their life through
"pretending it better"?

Yep! And we call them Masters.

The Universe

Sure beats pretending nothing is happening.

© www.tut.com

An enlightened soul

is not one to which truth has been revealed,
but one who has summoned it;
and not just when they've been driven by pain,
but when life's seas were as calm as glass.

The Universe

But you have to admit it's kind of handy that way, pain.
Just worked out like that. Honest.

© www.tut.com

JULY
JULIO
JUILLET

8

To err on the side of generosity,
patience, and kindness... is not to err.

No little thing slips by me,
which isn't returned BIGGER.

The Universe

© www.tut.com

JUNE
JUNIO
JUIN
26

I'm hungry. Hungry for adventure.
The adventure of love.

Tell you what: The more you give of it today
to the least deserving on your list,
the more your life will change.

Kindness is King.

The Universe

© www.tut.com

JULY
JULIO
JUILLET
7

It seems a shame that for many,
life doesn't seem fair.

But perhaps that's one of the reasons you were
summoned: To make life a little more bearable
for them, until they learn how fair it is
and can do the same for others.

The Universe

© www.tut.com

JUNE
JUNIO
JUIN
27

Release me, release me to do your will,
to move heaven and earth, to orchestrate
the players and summon the circumstances
that will change your life completely
by doing your all out best with today.

That's all the leg-up I need,
The Universe

© www.tut.com

Persistence is priceless,
but its value lies in doing, doing, doing;
not in waiting, waiting, waiting.

OK? OK? OK?

The Universe

Not that you were hanging around for someone,
someway, or somehow.

© www.tut.com

JUNE
JUNIO
JUIN
28

Do you know what's 1,000,000 times better
than being on top of the world?

Getting there, after having been lost.

Ohhh yeah,
The Universe

MapQuest® has nothing to do with it.

© www.tut.com

JULY
JULIO
JUILLET

5

Enjoy your thoughts, take time to visualize,
and meditate to soothe your soul.
But whatever you do, please don't forget
to spend a little energy, every single day,
physically doing stuff
and loving every second of it.

The Universe

© www.tut.com

JUNE
JUNIO
JUIN
29

As you've probably deduced by now,
I don't think in terms of reasonable or unreasonable,
likely or unlikely, possible or impossible.

I merely figure out the "hows."

Guess what that leaves you with?

The Universe

© www.tut.com

JULY
JULIO
JUILLET 4

You need never doubt that I tirelessly conspire
on your behalf. Because if it hasn't occurred to you yet,
I need you as much as you need me.
To show me the way, to give me each day,
and to go where I couldn't otherwise go.

The Universe

© www.tut.com

JUNE
JUNIO
JUIN
30

If you only knew

how many miracles you've already performed,
nothing would ever again overwhelm you,
frighten you, or seem impossible.

And you'd begin admiring yourself,
as we always have.

The Universe

© www.tut.com

JULY
JULIO
JUILLET
3

You know what's so strange about walking
that long, and oftentimes lonely, road of life?

When you reach its end, you won't remember
it being either long, or lonely.

The Universe

© www.tut.com

JULY
JULIO
JUILLET

1

If it wasn't for needing you there so much,
I'd need you here.

"Thanks," on behalf of all those in your life
right now who are just too busy, or stressed,
or sad to see how much you add to theirs.

The Universe

© www.tut.com

JULY
JULIO
JUILLET

2

The thing about success is that she often
arrives at such a late hour that only the odd balls,
freaks, and nuts (you know, the ones who continued
believing in spite of all worldly evidence to the contrary)
remain to greet her.

A little weird is good.

The Universe

© www.tut.com